The Refugees

Janice Marriott

illustrated by
Don DeMacedo

Learning Media

Chapter 1

This was the night I had to sneak out. I knew it was going to be difficult with all of us sleeping in one room at the front of the house. No one slept deeply now. Usually we slept for a while, then woke suddenly, fearful.

I waited. Our mother, wrapped in her quilt on the couch, turned over and angrily plumped up her pillow, then settled again. My big sister was asleep, her fingers twitching on her sleeping bag.

A whimper, then the shock of a baby's cry. Our mother carried our little sister out to the kitchen.

That was my chance. I took it.

I put my pillow inside the sleeping bag to look like me, then tiptoed to the front door and out into the yard. It was dark. There were no street lights – there was no electricity.

I felt under a bush for the sack I had hidden days ago. In the garage, I took down the spade.

I crept along the dark shadow of the wall, past the walnut tree, to where the earth was soft and sandy: Grandfather's asparagus bed.

I felt someone watching me. I looked around, but could see nothing in the dark. I listened. Silence.

I thought about our father, who was on neighborhood watch duty for the night. He'd be listening too – for marching feet, for trucks, for explosions. Alert for the smell of gasoline that warned of fire. I hoped he was safe.

I dug. The spade sounded like a whisper as it slid into the soil.

Faster. Deeper. Faster.
Deep enough.

I lowered the sack into the hole, scooped the soil back, and squatted to press it flat.

I crept back to the garage. As I replaced the spade, I heard something. A breath, just one. Someone *was* there! I froze. Footsteps, very soft, crept away.

I waited. I still had to get back across the gap between the garage and the house. I ran, zig-zagging expertly, using my soccer skills. I flung myself silently through the door. It was as though I was the ball, the door the goalposts.

The house was quiet. I'd made it. I was safe. But someone had been out there. Someone had watched the burial.

Chapter 2

Our mother was asleep again, with the baby curled under her chin. My big sister was asleep too. No one stirred as I slithered back into my sleeping bag. Outside, a dog howled, forlorn as a foghorn.

I tried not to worry about the person I'd heard outside. Instead, I shut my eyes and imagined scoring a goal from just outside the penalty box, at a game where my hero, the famous soccer star, was picking players for an under-14 side. I kicked hard, fast, and true. The ball bulleted toward the goal ….

Crash! Our front window exploded. Bottles shattered on the floor. Men shouted. Light arced off glass splinters. Soldiers, their faces cloaked by darkness behind their flashlights, broke large pieces of glass out of the frame and threw them down in front of them. Then they climbed in. Their boots crunched across the carpet.

My sister and I struggled in our sleeping bags to wiggle behind the couch. The men yanked our mother up by her hair. It unraveled and gleamed in the beam of light. She clutched the baby to her. Men pushed them both into the hall and through the front door. They marched them away.

I remember our mother's hand, bleeding, as she cradled our baby sister's head.

More soldiers smashed their way through the house. They poured gasoline over the books in the study and threw a match. Then they left. I was so frightened I couldn't move.

My sister pushed and dragged me outside, just ahead of the flames. She propped me up against the walnut tree. Then she threw rocks and bottles at the departing jeep. I burst into tears.

We hid in the garage and watched our house burn.

In the daylight, the first thing I noticed were the scorched leaves of the walnut tree our grandfather had planted long before we were born. Then I turned and saw that our house was a black, roofless shell.

I stayed in the garage all day, holding onto our old dog. My sister went out to search for our father, and for food.

"I found bread," she said, and divided it between us.

We didn't talk about what she hadn't found.

When it grew dark, neighbors began arriving to see what had happened to our family. They argued about what to do. Most people said that they were making for the hills.

"We have to go too," said my sister. "There's nothing left for us here."

I knew what she meant. I refused to believe it. "We can't leave!" I said.

"We must," she insisted. "Tonight."

Chapter 3

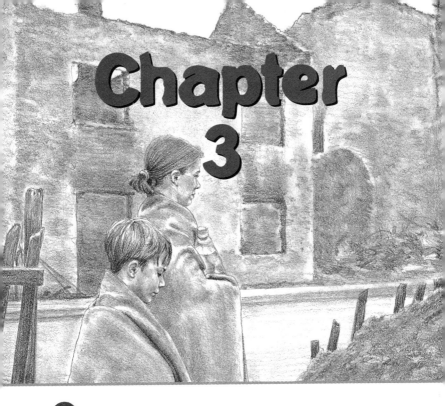

Our old dog wouldn't leave the ruined house.

"He's waiting for Dad," I said. I wanted to wait for him too.

"Come *on*!" my sister shouted at me.

We walked out of town, blankets wrapped around our shoulders. My sister had a plastic bottle of water and a flashlight that she'd found in the garage. I had nothing. I had buried the only things that mattered to me.

We stumbled along in the dark, climbing a steep road. We followed people. Others followed us. "Who are you?" someone whispered beside me.

I shook my head. Who *was* I? My name? Yes, I still had that. Address? No. I didn't have that anymore. School? No way. And parents? I swallowed hard. In my head, I practiced saying lightly, "They're not with us just now."

I ran ahead, away from the person who had asked the question I couldn't answer.

We trudged on and on. I knew I had no possessions now. It was like having no past at all. I stopped myself thinking about it. I made myself think about soccer instead. I invented a new self, ready for the next person who asked "Who are you?" With a furnace of anger inside me, I decided I could be anyone now, anyone at all. Even a soccer star.

I tripped over something in the road. I looked down. Was that a bunch of clothes or –

"Leave that!" my sister shouted. "Hurry up!"

We walked without stopping, for one night and one whole day. We kept climbing. No one organized us. No one led. No one spoke. There was no energy for talk.

My sister looked around at the burned-out buildings, the still-smoldering cars and trucks. She watched everything with the sharp eyes of the hunted. I tried to see no more than the heels in front of me.

At dusk on the second day, we shuffled into the shelter of an old quarry. There were cars loaded with people and their things.

Thirsty, hungry, shaking with exhaustion, we approached the man who seemed to be the boss. He reminded me of my soccer coach. When he asked, "Who are you?", I tried to tell him my new superstar identity. But no words came. Instead, I was filled with a memory of that coach I had loved. "Swing the leg back. Look where you want the ball to go. Kick. Look up. *Will* that ball to go up, up. Stay with it all the way!"

I took a deep breath to tell this stranger I was a soccer star, but the voice that replied to his question wasn't mine. It was my sister's big, sure voice, saying our names, our parents' names, their occupations, the name of the town we had lived in until yesterday.

"… and this is my little brother." She put her arm around me.

I hated my sister. I wasn't her little brother anymore. I was a totally different person now. She was ruining my plan.

"What can I do?" my sister asked the man after we had shared some of his food and water.

"Take a turn on watch duty," he replied.

"Stay here with me," I whispered. "Don't go."
I was suddenly afraid. "Don't leave me!"

"Toughen up," she muttered and walked away.

Chapter 4

There were days with no food. There was water that stung when you drank it.

My sister learned everything she could that would help us survive. She found food for us. When she kept watch, she noticed anything that moved between the trees in the valleys.

I noticed nothing. I lay curled on the ground, feeling like I'd been hit on the head. I wished I had been.

I met a girl, younger than me, and her little brother. They had joined up with a group of people, but really they had no one. I told them stories. It helped to pass the time. I told them about heroes catching villains and princes slaying dragons. I told them about magic stones that made soup and spells that meant that the porridge pot was never empty.

It was all I could do.

Once, an old woman tried to drag the children away to collect firewood for her. They didn't want to go with her. I stood up for them.

"Who do you think you are?" the old woman shouted at me.

This was my chance. "I'm a soccer star," I said.

She snorted and shook her head like a horse. But she left us alone.

"Tell us about being famous," the girl demanded.

So, while the adults foraged for food or tried to fix cars, I told the two children about my life as a soccer star. Three pairs of eyes shone as we forgot our fear and hunger for a while.

My sister interrupted the story. "Come with me," she said. "It's our turn to find food."

"Go away."

"If you don't come, we'll starve," she said. "I can't do it on my own."

My sister had found a village that hadn't been wrecked, half a day's walk away.

We hid near the village until nightfall. Then we raided the first house we found with an open window. My sister kept watch as I filled a sack with cans from a cupboard. I dropped one. We fled just as a woman ran downstairs. I remember her cry of rage and frustration as we bolted.

When we got back to the quarry, we shared the food around.

"Tomorrow we'll walk to the border," my sister announced.

"What about ....?" I looked at the two small children.

My sister turned away and didn't answer.

Chapter 5

It took us a week to get to the border. We walked. We hitched rides. Sometimes we carried the little boy. We didn't talk.

The soldier standing with the border guard had the bulkiest uniform we'd ever seen and a backpack made of the same camouflage material. He was covered in buckles, zippers, and pockets. "Spaceman!" said the little boy.

Nearby, there was a bunch of people speaking in a language we didn't understand. They had microphones, tape recorders, and video cameras. They all wore big silver watches.

"Who are they?" I asked my sister.

"The media," she said.

The four of us were put into a jeep. We were driven to a tent where people sat at tables with laptop computers and piles of notebooks and forms.

The "Who are you?" question was about to hit me again – this time in a strange language. I let my sister deal with it. I sat with the two little ones.

Mugs of something hot appeared. The whole world shrank into my mug. Nothing else existed for me. I could see my face in the liquid. My eye stared out at me. I stared back. "Do I know you?" I wondered. "Who are you?"

I drank, and my reflected eye disappeared. I kept my face in the mug so I wouldn't have to see all those strangers.

After we'd been written about in many notebooks and on many forms, we went for another long ride. Finally the jeep stopped. We were set down at a big tent, in a row of tents all the same. Our parents weren't there.

We clung to each other and cried then. All that walking. All that hunger. All that concentrating to keep out fear. Had we endured all that for a tent in a sea of mud?

We got used to the tents, the noise, the smells. We began to recognize the people around us.

The camp affected each of us differently. My sister admired the soldiers in the bulky uniforms – the peacekeepers. They were tall, smart, and powerful. They always had kids running along beside them.

I hated them. They were clean and happy. We were cold, ragged, dirty, and miserable. They were heroes. We were losers. I felt ashamed.

We looked for our parents differently too. My sister kept going to the processing tent and reading through the lists of names. She asked all the peacekeepers for help. There was never any news.

I wandered up and down the muddy lanes between the tents, looking into people's faces without letting anyone look at me. Once, I thought I saw our father slipping between two tents. But it wasn't him.

I stopped looking for them after that. It was too painful to hope.

I stopped trying to find my old self too. I became the soccer star, without a ball and without a team. I lay on my stretcher and told all the kids stories about cars, hotels, swimming pools, and piles and piles of food. They wanted to know how much I earned when I won a game and what happened if I lost. I told them it didn't matter if you won or lost, but they knew I didn't mean it. Winning was everything.

The two little ones came running up one day. They said my sister was organizing a soccer game among the kids in the camp. She had a ball that a cameraman had given her.

"You have to play!"

"Kick the biggest goal!"

"Beat them!"

I had to tell them I couldn't play soccer anymore because of a back injury. I curled up again on my stretcher. I longed to play, but I knew I could never play like a real soccer star – like my hero. I didn't want to disappoint them. We'd all had too much disappointment.

I felt terrible when I heard them playing outside. But I knew that we all needed my soccer star stories. Especially me.

Chapter 6

We stayed in that mucky camp for a month. One day there was feverish excitement. An important person was coming to visit. Some people cleaned up their tents. Hundreds of people stood in line for hours near the place marked for the helicopter's arrival.

At last, the sky thudded and shook. The helicopter appeared, swung to and fro, and descended. People cheered and shouted. I didn't know who the celebrity was – a politician, or a movie star, I guessed. When the helicopter door opened, some men and a woman ran toward us, bent over below the whirling blades. They looked beautiful, very clean, very neat. Someone threw handfuls of balloons out of the helicopter. All the kids fell on them as if they were food. We blew them up, tied knots in the necks, and waved them around.

My sister was leaping up and down, trying to attract the important person. The woman came toward us trailing her group of media people. She smiled and spoke kindly to us in her strange language. We didn't understand, but we cheered and clapped. The men shook hands with some of the cleaner children.

The media people, juggling their cameras and microphones, encouraged us to hold the balloons high around the smiling woman.

Then the glittering pack, with their cameras, microphones, and little telephones, ran back to the helicopter. It rose slowly, swaying, into the air and thudded away. We stood in the mud and watched until it disappeared.

Who were those people? Why did they come? It was as unreal as a visit from angels.

My sister talked to many people that night. I stomped around the tent, bursting balloons. What use is a balloon? You can't even kick it.

The little kids disappeared that day. My sister said that their parents must have found them. I hoped it was true.

The days stretched out. I stopped telling stories about heroes and dragons. I didn't even tell stories about being a soccer star anymore. Somehow superstars didn't mean anything to me now that I'd seen that media star.

My sister started talking to the media people. She borrowed a phrase book and learned some of their language. We argued. She said she wanted to get on every TV in the world, in case our parents were out there somewhere.

"It's not possible!" I shouted. I hated her for not giving up hope.

Then a rumor lifted each tent flap and blew through the camp like a hurricane.

"It can't be!" people said.

"Are you sure?"

But the rumor was true – the war was over. We cheered.

"What happens next?" someone asked.

It seemed as if the announcement should be followed by a sudden time warp. We would magically be back in our homes with our families. Life would go back to normal.

But it wasn't like that. The war was over, but we were still in the camp. Our house was still burned. Our parents and baby sister were still missing.

Later, we were all told we could go home. Again there were cheers.

At first I was glad too. Then the panic started. How could we get home? How would we live? Who would look after us?

"I don't want to go," I told my sister.

"Some of our things might still be there," she said, looking hard at me.

I remembered the buried sack then. I wanted it, badly.

"Come on," said my sister. "Let's go home." She held out her hand.

Chapter 7

Crushed in back of a truck, we returned to our home town. We walked the last miles to our suburb, our street. There was no traffic. We hiked past the husks of houses. Everything smelled of burning. A pile of tires still smoldered. I coughed. It was the only sound.

We turned the corner and there, across the sky, pointed the blackened limbs of Grandfather's walnut tree. I remembered him telling me it took twenty years for that tree to bear fruit. It wouldn't bear walnuts again.

There was no sign of our parents. I slowed down. My sister started running. I saw her kick in the splintered garage door, and then she was out again, shouting, "The spade! It's not there!"

So? Why did she want the spade? She started scrabbling in the dirt near the tree. What was she …?

Then I knew.

"Leave that alone!" I shouted, running toward her. I jumped on her back and tried to pull her away. She fought back. She twisted my arm behind me.

"Let go!" I screamed.

"What did you bury here?"

"Nothing!"

She threw me aside and started digging with her hands again.

I hated her.

I sat under the dead tree, not watching. For me, it was one of the worst moments of the war.

I heard her grunting with the effort, cursing because she wasn't sure exactly where to dig.

I shut my eyes. Then I heard this roar, like a dog's howl. Cold poured through me. I got up and started to run away.

My sister ran after me, shouting. She caught up with me, grabbed me.

"Where's the money?" she roared, shaking me. "Mother's jewelry? The silverware?"

"I didn't ...."

"What was the use of burying that – that *junk*!"

She was crying as she hurled me aside and ran around the side of the charred house.

I walked over to the hole she'd dug. There, beside the dirty sack, was my old toybox, lying open, its contents spilling out.

There were the family photos.

There was the walnut, the seed of Grandfather's tree.

There was my certificate for making the school's soccer team.

There was my scrapbook of clippings about my soccer hero.

These were all the things I'd buried that night when I felt something terrible could happen. These were my most important possessions. These were the things that answered the question "Who are you?" These things were *me*.

I squashed them all back in the box and shut the lid, unable to look at any of it.

Chapter 8

The garage still had a roof. It became our home.

That first night, our old dog showed up. He was thin, with crazy eyes, but he curled up beside us. It was so good to see him. My sister started to plan how she could train him to hunt. I just wanted to hold him.

My sister said, "I have an idea. Wait here for me."

"Don't leave me!" I said. But she was gone.

I opened the old toybox for comfort. I still couldn't look at the family photos, but I needed to know they were there, safe. I looked at the walnut and the soccer star pictures. That night, I fell asleep with the box in my arms and the old dog for a pillow.

A day later my sister returned with a TV crew.

"Why?" I couldn't understand it. "What are they here for?"

"The soccer scrapbook," she said. "Show them."

I thought my sister had gone crazy, but I handed it over. It was the least precious thing in the box now.

The TV people loved it. They filmed it. They filmed the toybox. They filmed the hole it was buried in and our burned house. Then they left.

My sister said the story would bring the soccer star. "It'll be a publicity thing for him," she said. "And if they interview you, you can ask if anyone knows where our parents are!"

"No!" I shouted at her. "I can't do it. I won't!" I hated the way my sister wouldn't give up hoping. She wouldn't admit we were losers.

"You will!" she shouted back, and she shook me. "You *will*! Because it's our only hope of getting our family back!"

I kicked her. I was hot with anger. But I felt something waken in me – some seed of hope that hadn't quite been crushed. And immediately I had a better plan.

"*You* do it," I said. "*You* be the kid who buried the soccer star's photos. I won't tell. You'd do it better than me." Finally she agreed.

For two days we wandered around the neighborhood, planning what she would say. My sister kept looking upward. "They'll come from the sky," she said.

She was right.

On the third day, a pulse beat in the sky. We ran for cover as the helicopter landed in the road. A film crew leaped out, and then there he was – in a clean, bright track suit, carrying an autographed ball. The soccer star. My hero.

I hid in the garage. I was sick with embarrassment. I didn't even like the soccer star anymore.

Chapter 9

I watched it all from the garage.

One man stood with feet planted on the rubble, camera on shoulder. Another man wrote in a notebook. A young woman fussed around the soccer star, combing his hair and dabbing powder on his nose.

My sister put on my dreams. She showed the interviewer where she'd buried the sack. She showed the box and the scrapbook of pictures of the soccer star. She looked at the star all the time as she spoke, but he just kept looking at the pretty translator. My sister said she'd always slept with the soccer star's photo under her pillow before the war. She said she loved playing soccer. She said she dreamed of being a soccer star.

Then my sister showed photos of our parents and our baby. She told the world how badly we needed to know what had happened to them. She said we wanted them to know we were all right. She said we'd be here, waiting.

She was fantastic.

In the dark, charred garage, I interviewed myself. "Who are you?" I am a refugee. A person without a home. But I have a mother, a father, and a baby sister – somewhere. Dead or alive, they are my family. And I have a big sister, right here. And I love her.

Once I had a hero, a soccer star, who ruled my life. Not now. Now I dream of living life again. I dare to hope.

The soccer star, the interviewer, the translator, the makeup person and the film crew all piled back into the helicopter. They promised to keep in touch. They promised to look for our parents. The soccer star promised tickets to his next game. Most important, they promised that the interview with my sister would be on the world news. Then they were gone.

That was yesterday. Today, we wait.

We wait for our parents, or someone who knows what's happened to them, to see that interview on television. Or for someone in the other, richer, less troubled world to invite us into their family.

We also wait for our tickets to the soccer star's next game. But we're not holding our breath.

While we wait, we play soccer among the ruins with other survivors.

I kick a great shot, over the washing lines that are somehow still standing. The ball arcs up, up, into the blue. My hopes curve with it through the sky.

"Stay with the ball," I hear my coach say. "Follow it right to the goal!"

I will. I'll never stop hoping.

The ball lands in the goal. We all cheer. "Good one!" my sister shouts.

And we continue our waiting game.